W9-AYW-512

Rough Guides

25 Ultimate experiences

Journeys

Make the most of your time on Earth

ROUGH GUIDES

25 YEARS 1982–2007

NEW YORK • LONDON • DELHI

Contents

Introduction

EXPERIENCES have always been at the heart of the Rough Guide concept. A group of us began writing the books **25 years ago** (hence this celebratory mini series) and wanted to share the kind of travels we had been doing ourselves. It seems bizarre to recall that in the early 1980s, travel was very much a minority pursuit. Sure, there was a lot of tourism around, and that was reflected in the guidebooks in print, which traipsed around the established sights with scarcely a backward look at the local population and their life. We wanted to change all that: to put a country or a city's popular culture centre stage, to highlight the clubs where you could hear local music, drink with people you hadn't come on holiday with, watch the local football, join in with the festivals. And of course we wanted to push travel a bit further, inspire readers with the confidence and knowledge to break away from established routes, to find pleasure and excitement in remote islands, or desert routes, or mountain treks, or in street culture.

Twenty-five years on, that thinking seems pretty obvious: we all want to experience something real about a destination, and to seek out travel's **ultimate experiences**. Which is exactly where these **25 books** come in. They are not in any sense a new series of guidebooks. We're happy with the series that we already have in print. Instead, the **25s** are a collection of ideas, enthusiasms and inspirations: a selection of the very best things to see or do – and not just before you die, but now. Each selection is gold dust. That's the brief to our writers: there is no room here for the average, no space fillers. Pick any one of our selections and you will enrich your travelling life.

But first of all, take the time to browse. Grab a half dozen of these books and let the ideas percolate … and then begin making your plans.

Mark Ellingham
Founder & Series Editor, Rough Guides

25

Ultimate
experiences
Journeys

Packing a few belongings into the trunk of your car and hitting the road to roll hundreds of miles across open prairie or along urban seaboards is arguably the quintessential American experience. Numerous cross-country road-trip routes are writ large in the nation's folklore, but Highway 1 stands head and hard shoulders above the rest: a 550-mile ribbon of gleaming tarmac that hugs the Pacific as it careers from Northern California's redwood forests to the sunny beaches of LA.

01 **California in a Convertible:**
Driving the Length of Highway 1

Highway 1 starts in little Leggett, but most people pick it up in San Francisco, just after it has raced US-101 across the Golden Gate Bridge and wiggled its way through the city. Roll down the rooftop on your convertible – this is California, after all – and chase the horizon south, through Santa Cruz and misty Monterey and then on to Big Sur, one of the most dramatic stretches of coastline in the world, where the forest-clad foothills of the Santa Lucia Mountains ripple down to a ninety-mile zigzag of deeply rugged shore.

You could easily spend a week in one of the mountain lodges here, hiking in the region's two superb state parks or watching grey whales gliding through the surf, but SoCal's sands are calling. Gun the gas down through San Luis Obispo and swanky Santa Barbara until you hit Malibu, from where – as the Pacific Coast Highway – the road tiptoes around Los Angeles, dipping in and out of the beachside suburbs of Santa Monica, Venice and Long Beach.

Highway 1 eventually peters out at San Juan Capistrano, but most people pull off a few miles shy, finishing their journey in Los Angeles. Leaving Malibu's multi-million-dollar condos behind and easing gently into the downtown LA traffic, it'll suddenly dawn on you that the hardest part of the journey is still to come – at some point soon, you're going to have to say goodbye to the convertible.

need to know

Several major tour operators offer fly-drive deals to California. To experience life on the road in true Golden State-style, rent a convertible; you can slip behind the wheel of a Chevrolet Corvette for £170/$320 per day with San Francisco-based Specialty Rentals (@www.specialtyrentals.com).

A night on the equator with Kenya Railways

Constructed in the 1890s, Kenya's "Lunatic Line" (so named by the British press for the folly of building a line into the unexplored interior of Africa) has come to be one of Africa's best-loved train journeys.

Your London-style cab pulls into the forecourt of Nairobi's scruffy but civilized railway station and an elderly porter beats his colleagues to the door. Minutes later, installed in your compartment, you feel the train pull out –7pm sharp; outside it is pitch dark.

Just after departure, a steward in a shiny-buttoned, frayed, white tunic strides through the carriages ringing a bell – time for dinner: a kind of do-it-yourself version of silver service accompanied by waiters leaning with wobbling plates of tomato soup, tilapia fish and curry. So begins your 526km overnight journey across the savannah to the island city of Mombasa.

Every evening one diesel train pulls out of the capital bound for the coast and another leaves in the opposite direction. Give or take five minutes – and a suitably synchronized passing at the only stretch of double line in the middle – each train arrives at the other end at 9am.

Outside, with Nairobi's shanties left behind, the big, dark spaces begin. You peer in to the nocturnal emptiness of the plains, where Maasai and Akamba herders traipse by day, tending their cattle among zebra, wildebeest, giraffe and ostrich, and you make a mental note to keep your eyes peeled over breakfast on the return journey. Back at your compartment, beds have been made up and sleep, with the incessant rocking of the carriage, comes quickly.

In the mild, grey light of pre-dawn, you awake to an awareness that the climate has changed: you're out of the 5000-foot highlands and dropping to the Indian Ocean coast. As you twist on your bunk to stare out of the window, tropical odours and humidity percolate through the carriages, together with a fresh brew of coffee. The equatorial sun rises as fast as it set and as the train jolts at walking speed through the suburbs of Mombasa. With prayer calls in the air and Indian sweet shops on the streets, you disembark, already seduced by the coast's beguiling combination of Asia, Africa and Arabia.

need to know: The train currently runs three times a week in each direction, though new management is expected to restore the daily service. Book locally (1st class $45) or in advance with an agent, for example Ⓦwww.eastafricashuttles.com/train.htm, for a supplementary fee.

You're only going to do this once, so do it right and see it all. Across the tropical north from Cape Leveque, Western Australia to Cape York on Queensland's northern tip, it's a two-month, 8000-kilometre adventure via the Northern Territory's striking Central Deserts. Broome, on the dazzling turquoise Indian Ocean is a great place to start, right beside the pearly sands of Cable Beach. The journey kicks off with the suspension-mashing 700-kilometre Gibb River Road; starting near Derby, it cuts through the Kimberley region's untamed ranges, known as Australia's "Alaska". Along the way, turn-offs tempt you to idyllic waterfalls like the Bell Creek Gorge where water rolls off a series of ledges into shallow inviting pools. The Gibb finally spits you out at Kununurra township, where you can stock up on provisions and, hopefully, team up with another vehicle for the stretch ahead. Now comes the lonely 1500-kilometre all-dirt stage into the Territory and down to Alice Springs, notable for the only traffic lights en route until Cairns

Exploring Alice's hinterland and weaving among the majestic ghost gum trees along the shady Finke River track to Uluru (Ayers Rock) is an adventure in itself. Moving on from the Rock, scoot eastwards to the solitary Mt Dare homestead; fill up here and then head out across the dune fields of the Simpson Desert to join the pilgrimage to the legendarily remote *Birdsville Hotel*, Australia's best known bush pub.

Have a drink, then head any which way northeast across Queensland's flat dusty interior. It's time to get ready for the 1000-kilometre creek-crossing climax of your journey: the "Trip to the Tip". Between you and the Pacific lies one of the most ecologically diverse habitats on the planet: creeper-draped rainforest teeming with tombstone anthills and dayglo snakes.

Watching the sunset over Cape York, your journey is complete; the red dust is now in your blood and what you've missed of the Australian outback is a very short list indeed.

need to know

For a long trip you're best buying a 4WD bushcamper for around Aus20,000. Visit @www.exploreoz.com for good advice and information on outback four-wheeling.

OCEAN TO
OCEAN,
CAPE TO
CAPE:

ACROSS
AUSTRALIA
BY 4WD

Cycling for the Soul:

Traditionally, pilgrimage meant hoofing it, wayfaring the hard way. Yet most Catholic authorities will tell you there's nothing particularly sinful about making it easier on yourself. You could roughly trace Spain's *Camino de Santiago*, or Way of St James, by car... but then taking full advantage of the fringe benefits – discount accommodation and gorgeous red wine – would prove difficult. The answer? Get on your bike.

With reasonable fitness and not a little tenacity, the mantra of two wheels good four wheels bad can take you far, on a religious pilgrimage route that pretty much patented European tourism back in the Middle Ages. The most popular section begins at the Pyrenean Monastery of Roncesvalles, rolling right across northwestern Spain to the stunning (and stunningly wet) Galician city of Santiago de Compostela, where the presence of St James' mortal remains defines the whole exercise. Pack your mac, but spare a thought for the pre-Gortex, pre-Penny Farthing millions who tramped through history, walking 500 miles to lay down at Santiago's door.

Bikers can expect a slight spiritual snag: 200km to qualify for a purgatorial reprieve (twice the minimum for walkers), but by the time you're hurtling down to Pamplona with a woody-moist Basque wind in your hair, purgatory will be the last thing on your mind. Granted, the vast, windswept plains between Burgos and León have greater potential for torment but by then you'll have crossed the Ebro and perhaps taken a little detour to linger amongst the vineyards of La Rioja, fortifying your weary pins with Spain's most acclaimed wine.

The *Camino* was in fact responsible for spreading Rioja's reputation, as pilgrims used to slake their thirst at the monastery of Santo Domingo de la Calzada. The medieval grapevine likewise popularized the Romanesque architecture for which the route is celebrated; today many of the monasteries, convents and churches house walkers and cyclists. Once you're past the Cebreiro pass and into Celtic-green Galicia, rolling past hand-ploughed plots and slate-roofed villages, even a bike will seem new-fangled amidst rhythms that have scarcely changed since St James's remains first turned up in 813.

need to know

Credencials (or Pilgrim's Passport) are available from Roncesvalles Monastery for a few euros, entitling you to free or very cheap hostal accommodation. Allow 2–3 weeks.

05 Taking the A-Train through Manhattan

It may be just a dirty, run-of-the-mill inner-city commuter train, but ever since 1941 when Duke Ellington immortalized the A-train – the subway from Brooklyn up through the heart of Manhattan and into Harlem – the route's been associated with jazz, the Harlem Renaissance and the gritty glamour of travelling through New York. The iconic tin-can carriages – long a favourite location for television cop dramas – rattle along on this express route, taking you to some of Manhattan's most varied neighbourhoods.

Wherever you choose to board the train, getting out at Jay Street in Brooklyn Heights, and stopping at one of the cafés on leafy Montague Street for a long, lazy brunch starts the day in true New York style. From here, the Brooklyn Bridge beckons; cross on foot and enter downtown Manhattan, taking in the spectacular views of the skyline as you traverse the sparkling East River, the Statue of Liberty just visible to your left.

Rejoin the A-train at Park Place and head up the line. Jump off at West 4th Street and browse the boutiques alongside funky West Villagers; stop at Columbus Circle, emerging at the southwest corner of Central Park for a leafy stroll. From here it's a non-stop express trip whizzing under the Upper West Side – sit in the front carriage for a driver's eye view of the glinting tracks as they disappear beneath the train.

Your final stop is Duke Ellington's own journey's end: 145th Street for Harlem's Sugar Hill. High above the city, with hazy views back along Manhattan's straight avenues, this was the more upmarket part of the neighbourhood during the Jazz Age. Today, well into its second renaissance, the area's art and music scenes thrive, nowhere so much as in its classic jazz clubs. Stick your head into **St Nick's Pub**, known to the greats as **Lucky's Rendezvous**, and catch some improv – Duke would definitely approve.

way

need to know

The A-train runs from Queens through Brooklyn and Manhattan to Inwood–207th Street; during the day, it's an express through Manhattan stopping only at stations marked on the maps with white dots, rather than the usual black. A single trip costs $2; a one-day MetroCard $7.
St Nick's Pub is at 773 St Nicholas Ave, corner of 149th St.

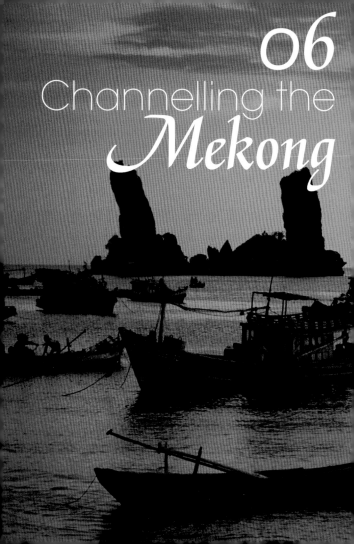

06
Channelling the *Mekong*

It was the Mekong that drew some of the earliest French explorers to Laos – eager to find a backdoor route to the riches of inner China. But pesky rapids, waterfalls and shallow waters made the river navigable only in parts and poor old Laos had to settle for second-class status among France's colonies. Perhaps it was all for the best – hop aboard one of the rickety wooden boats that ply the river today, and you'll soon be slipping past wild, verdant landscapes that haven't changed for decades.

Lifeline of this remote, landlocked nation, the Mekong links the northern highland home of the Akha and Hmong peoples to the capital, Vientiane, and eventually to the ethnic Lao communities of the Four Thousand Islands in the far south. Over the course of its two-thousand-kilometre journey, the river eases past thousand-year-old Khmer ruins and riverside towns dotted with crumbling French villas, before crashing over the series of waterfalls that dashed the hopes of the French explorers and finally rushing off toward Cambodia.

Today, you can still cruise the Mekong in traditional Lao style: board one of the veritable armada of jury-rigged passenger boats in the town of Houay Xai and prepare for a long, slow ride. Within minutes of casting off, the captain eases his improbable wooden cigar of a vessel around a bend, and you're swallowed up by a sea of sawtoothed, purple-green mountains rolling off in every direction. En route, you'll pass fisherfolk setting bamboo traps among the river's sandbars and jagged rocks, beaches dotted with kids joyously shouting greetings "   " and ramshackle villages carved out of thick forests, days' walk from the nearest road. Two days and another bend in the river later, the setting sun catches a golden spire atop a hill in the old royal city of   , and you're back in civilization. Maybe there were riches up that river after all.

need to know

Passenger boats run year round along the Mekong's two main routes in Laos: from Houay Xai to Louang Phabang in the north (2 days; $22, overnight in Pakbeng not included), and from Pakse to Si Phan Don in the south (8–10hr; $5). The boats are very basic – bring your own food and drink.

need to know

The route described here is a **700km journey** and takes about four to five days at an easy pace. You can take an organized tour from Iquique but it's far more exciting to **hire a sturdy 4WD pickup truck** and drive it yourself. You'll need to carry all your petrol in **jerry cans** as there are no petrol stations along the way, and be sure to take **two spare tyres**, a good supply of **5-litre water bottles**, a tent and stove and plenty of food.

07 *Driving Through* THE ALTIPLANO

For those unfazed by appalling dirt roads, stray llamas and a singular lack of road signs, a drive through the Chilean altiplano makes for an unforgettable trip. **A high plateau connecting the eastern and western ranges of the Andes**, the altiplano is shared by several neighbouring countries – but nowhere is the getting there more dramatic than in Chile, where your journey starts right by the ocean, passes through a desert and winds up **4500m above sea level**.

Starting in the coastal town of Iquique in Chile's far north, the first leg of the journey takes you through the flat, scorched *pampa* of **the Atacama Desert** – a seemingly endless expanse of dull yellow and brown. Just when you think you'll never get out of this flat wasteland, you'll start climbing, gently at first, into **the foothills of the Andes**. A few hours later you're high in the mountains, in **a world of turquoise lakes, snow-capped volcanoes and thin, freezing air**. Beautiful and desolate in equal measure, the altiplano is sparsely populated by dwindling numbers of **indigenous Aymara** people, who've herded llamas up here for centuries; their **semi-abandoned villages** (most people now make their living in Iquique, only returning to their home villages for festivals and funerals), with whitewashed churches, make a striking sight.

For the ultimate altiplano experience, turn off the main road just before you hit the Bolivian border and take a bumpy ride north through **Parque Nacional Isluga** and onto **Parque Nacional Lauca** – your reward will be an **extravaganza of salt flats, hot springs, volcanoes and wildlife**. From Lauca you can head back down to civilization, ending your epic journey back by the ocean at the lively beach resort city of Arica, near the Peruvian border.

Trial by Trolleybus:
SIMFEROPOL TO YALTA

597

08

Bounce bounce. Squeak squeak. I've got an elbow in my ear, an unknown child in my lap and the cardboard box wedged under my seat, taking up all my legroom, is making strange cheeping noises. Of course there are easier ways of getting to the seaside. On the other hand, the Simferopol–Yalta trolleybus route in Crimea, at 86 kilometres and 742 metres – over the Angarskiy pass – is the world's longest and highest trolleybus line, so this journey is an event in itself. I wonder if the rest of the jam-packed passengers, clinging on for dear life round hair-raising bends, are also consoling themselves with that fact.

The line was completed in 1961 to ferry Soviet holidaymakers from the rail terminal at Simferopol to the Black Sea coast. I'm lucky enough to ride in a pleasingly rotund Škoda 9Tr, one of the original trolleybus fleet. There are bizarre, yet characterful moments when the trolleybus poles come unattached from the overhead electric wires and the driver has to get out and haul them back into place using ropes, a process not unlike a kind of upside-down fishing.

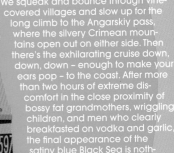

We squeak and bounce through vine-covered villages and slow up for the long climb to the Angarskiy pass, where the silvery Crimean mountains open out on either side. Then there's the exhilarating cruise down, down, down – enough to make your ears pop – to the coast. After more than two hours of extreme discomfort in the close proximity of bossy fat grandmothers, wriggling children, and men who clearly breakfasted on vodka and garlic, the final appearance of the satiny blue Black Sea is nothing short of miraculous. Salty breezes blow in through the windows, and I find I'm almost sorry to reach Yalta. I give up the child – to whom I've become rather attached – and can't resist asking the owner of the squeaking box under my seat what on earth is in there. It's full of cheeping fluffy yellow chicks. I'm still wondering why he was taking them to the seaside.

need to know: Trolleybus #52 runs about every 20 minutes from Simferopol railway station, and takes 2.5 hours. A one-way ticket costs 10 gryvnas (about US$2 or £1).

09

Across the Great Karoo

Take on the 1400-kilometre drive between Cape Town and Johannesburg and you'll discover there's an awful lot of nothing in South Africa's interior. This vast, semi-desert is called the Great Karoo, meaning "place of thirst", and it stretches from the southwestern Cape Mountains northeast to the Orange River. The name is apt: summer heat is fierce here, and the winter cold is biting; rain is elusive and the soil is all but barren. Slow creaking windmills struggle to bring water to the surface and the baked, brown-red earth is roamed only by skittish knots of springbok or small merino sheep. Few are the human inhabitants and those that do brave the desolation live on remote farms or huddled in squat, whitewashed settlements which seem to drift like rafts in an arid ocean.

You can – and most do – speed along the straight, featureless N1 highway at a steady 120 km/h. Every few hours you'll come upon a sterile service station offering some shade, a refrigerated drink and the chance to scrape the accumulated layers of insects from your front windscreen.

Do what few do and stop somewhere in the vastness; the total emptiness is quite awe-inspiring. Sitting in the shade of their verandahs, locals will tell you that after a few days, or maybe weeks, you'll come to relish the crispness of the air, the orange and ochre colours of the rocks on the flat-topped hills at sunset and the tenacious succulents and desert flowers that defy the heat and drought. There are few places on earth where you can see so much sky; at night, there are so many stars that even the familiar constellations get lost in the crowded galaxies. The water-starved Karoo is called Great for a reason.

need to know

It takes about 12 hours to drive between Cape Town and Jo'burg on the N1. The tiny towns of Richmond and Hanover are roughly halfway and are worth considering for a stop-over to sample a little of slow-paced life under a hot sun and big sky.
ⓦwww.northerncape.org.za.

25

The medieval city of Timbuktoo, clinging to life between Saharan dunes and an ancient loop of the Niger River, has always held a certain mystique. The name alone conjures resonant images of the **camel caravans and gold merchants** of its heyday. Yet today, its glory days long faded, Timbuktoo still retains its appeal as a destination, largely because of its physical isolation – **getting here is always a challenge**.

Taking the easiest approach via Mali's main road – a narrow strip of tarmac that runs across the plains – we halt at the truck-stop of Douentza. Here, over **a bowl of rice and sauce** we ask everyone we see about "transport à Tombouctou". In fine West African style, something is bound to turn up.

The next day, at sunrise, the hotel night watch raps on our door to tell us we have a lift, and within minutes we're in a Land Rover, driven by a former Tuareg rebel commander, thrashing up the gravel road north in the coolness of dawn. **The day unfolds in a blur of dust**, bouncing suspension and shuddering halts as the "road" dissolves periodically into a plait of sandy tracks. We pass Tuareg encampments and **groups of camels, hobbled to stop them straying**. Near a Fula shepherd camp, we stop to make tea in the roasting, silent noontime, breaking twigs from the acacia giving us shade to coax a tiny fire. **A girl brings us a calabash of goat's milk** – traditional rules of hospitality still apply.

Early in the afternoon, we pitch over a gentle rise, and there is the Niger, fronted by a great flat apron of dried mud beach to cross before we fetch up by the ferry embarkation point. Ten minutes up the avenue on the other side, we reach the entrance to the city. While **the mosques, sandy streets and markets are beguiling**, it's the sense of achievement we feel at simply getting here, and having our passports stamped at the tourist office – where they welcome each visitor with a warm handshake – that really leaves an impression.

need to know

You can also reach Timbuktoo along the river, by outboard or punted pinasse (a boat resembling a large canoe, which takes up to a week from Mopti) or by one of the few diesel riverboats when the water is high enough (Aug–Jan; 36–48hr from Mopti). There are also flights, several times a week, by light aircraft from Bamako.

10 Getting to Timbuktoo

Caledonian pines mirrored in still lochs glide by, heathery hills stretch out ahead of you and white-sand beaches dot the swiftly passing coastline. And if the scenery isn't romantic enough, the magnificent **Jacobite Steam Train** on which you're riding provides ample atmosphere; clouds of steam pour from the funnel of the **slick black engine** and the **liveried carriages** are pleasingly old-fashioned.

Steaming out of Fort William, the train passes **the mighty bulk of Ben Nevis**, the highest mountain in Britain at 1344m; you soon **cross the Caledonian Canal at Neptune's Staircase**, an impressive series of eight locks that turns the tranquil canal into something resembling a stepped waterfall. Just under an hour later, and nearly halfway into the journey, the train crosses the twenty-one arches of the lofty Glenfinnan viaduct, instantly recognizable to Harry Potter fans. Looking down to the left you'll see the **Glenfinnan Monument** on the banks of Loch Sheil, where the doomed Jacobite rebellion began in 1745; a statue of a clansman gazing out across the water tops the slender column of the monument. From here on the train runs through **the spectacular mountains and glens of the Rough Bounds**, before emerging, as you draw closer to Mallaig, at the pale sands of the intricately indented coast.

If you are lucky, you'll have **wonderful views of the islands** from here: hilly little Eigg, Rùm and the **great sharp pinnacles of Skye's Cuillin mountains**. Of course, whether you see anything other than rain lashing against the train's windows is a matter of chance – this is Scotland after all.

need to know
The service runs from June to mid-October; book on ☎01463/239026, ⊛www.steamtrain.info. The first leg of the West Highland Railway takes you from Glasgow to Fort William (but on ordinary trains).

11 The West Highland Railway: **Fort William to Mallaig**

Known to many as the "Harry Potter train" since its starring role as the Hogwart's Express, the West Highland Railway chugs its way through miles of wonderfully wild Scottish scenery, rich in associations with Bonnie Prince Charlie and the Highland uprising.

Over a hundred years after the initial exploration of the continent, journeying to Antarctica still feels like stepping off the known world. Take a cruise to the crooked finger of land which points northward to South America and you'll encounter the other-planetary landscape and mysterious draw of this land beyond time – for the most part still beyond civilization's reach.

Once through the Drake Passage – reputed to be the roughest body of water in the world – you feel the frozen land long before you actually see it. As you cross the invisible line of the Antarctic Convergence, a ribbon of coldwater current which circumnavigates the continent, the temperature plummets. Huge tabular icebergs appear – interpreting their fantastic shapes is at least half the fun. In the Gerlache Strait, sudden charcoal tors soar vertically from the water up to 1500ft and glaciers tumble vertically into the sea. From the ship you can brush against their hummocked layers of ice and try your hand at cataloguing their colours: cobalt, indigo and mint.

The tar-black Antarctic water teems with marine life: Humpback and Killer whales are fairly common, and if there

Voyage into the Icy Unknown: Cruising the Antarctic Peninsula

12

is sea-ice around you are guaranteed to see the silver-gold Crabeater and nonchalant Weddell seals who can hardly be bothered to vacate a floe even as the ship splits it in two. Myriad penguins emit a serenade of squawks as the ship passes and Albatrosses and Petrels are stalwart chaperones, flying level with the ship for days at a stretch.

Go ashore at the abandoned British Base B at Deception Island, flattened by a volcanic eruption, and the British Antarctic museum at Port Lockroy, where a preserved-in-aspic 1950s base is on display, complete with tinned fruitcake and rice pudding from the explorer era.

On the whole, however, the Antarctic is a monumentally empty place, and a cruise down the peninsula gives you only a glimpse of this uninhabited continent, larger than Australia – but it's enough to draw you in. Even as it emits a froideur, there is an odd magnetism to the Antarctic; you'll feel its pull long after you've left.

need to know: Regular cruise ships depart from early November to late March from Ushaia in Argentina or Punta Arenas in Chile; most cruises last between 8 and 22 days. For a variety of cruises and itineraries, go online at ⊛www.quarkexpeditions.com, ⊛www.antarpply.com and ⊛www. responsibletravel.com.

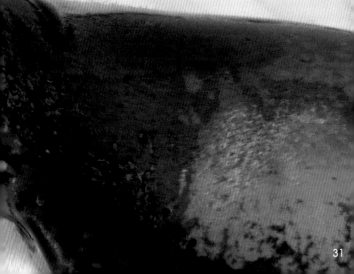

The Panama Canal, a narrow channel surrounded by virgin jungles teeming with toucans and white-faced capuchin monkeys, only takes a day to traverse. But during that day you'll experience an amazing feat of engineering and cross the continental divide between two of the world's great oceans. Politically fraught from its inception and burdened by the death of nearly thirty thousand workers during its construction, the 80km canal, opened in 1914, is a controversial yet fascinating waterway which offers safe passage to over 14,000 vessels per year.

Your trip begins in the Caribbean near the rough-and-tumble town of Colón, which prospered during the canal's construction but has since declined, its ramshackle colonial buildings and hand-painted signs frozen in time. Once on board, ships enter the narrow Gatun locks; the canal rises over 25 metres above sea level as it crosses the Panamanian isthmus, so you start and end your journey in a series of locks which elevate and then lower you from the ocean on either end.

need to know

Fares for day cruises from Colón City to Balboa port start at US$210; major cruise lines also operate tours departing from Panama City in the cooler months of September through June. For more information visit ⓦwww.pancanal.com/eng/panama/cruises.html or ⓦwww.ecoventures-travel.com.

From sea to shining sea:
Cruising the Panama Canal

On the far side, the enormous, sparkling Gatun Lake was formed by a flooded jungle valley and serves as an intersection for shipping freighters, cruise ships, local pleasure boaters and environmentalists, drawn by the lake's isolated islands – basically the tops of mountains that remained above water level. They and the surrounding rainforest are home to thousands of species of wildlife, including monkeys, sloths, lizards and a variety of tropical birds, all of which you'll see from the boat.

With the lake behind you, you enter the narrowest part of the canal – the Gaillard Cut. Blasted out of solid rock and shale mountainside, this channel is so perilously close that it's impossible for two large ships to pass; as you enter, your clothes stick to your skin in the hot, heavy equatorial air, the rainforest feels very close by. Listen for the calls of the myriad birds, loud and distinct above the engine's low-speed hum, and scan the banks, where you'll pick out crocodiles floating menacingly in the shallows.

After nearly 14km of slow, careful progress, you emerge at the Miraflores Locks, beyond which lies the Pacific. As you exit the final chamber and pass under the Bridge of the Americas at Balboa, the bright lights and skyscrapers of Panama City appear on your left. From the timeworn streets of Colón to the bustling metropolis ahead, you have truly travelled from one side of the world to the other.

A sleek, space-age train glides into the station precisely on time. When it pulls to a stop the doors align exactly in front of each orderly queue of passengers. The guard, wearing immaculate white gloves and a very natty peaked cap, bows as you climb aboard. Where but Japan could a train journey start in such style?

Japan's high-speed Shinkansen, popularly known as the bullet train, is the envy of the world, and while it's not cheap, it's something you just have to do once. The Tokaido-Sanyo line runs from Tokyo west to Kyoto and Hiroshima – 900km – and the fastest "Nozomi" trains cover this in just four hours. In places, they reach 300km per hour, yet the ride is as smooth as silk.

It's only by looking out of the window that you get a sense of speed; neat rows of houses flicker by, gradually giving way to rice fields, woods and the occasional temple, as you leave Tokyo's sprawling metropolis behind. If the weather's clear, you'll catch Mount Fuji's iconic, snow-capped cone.

need to know: The Japan Rail Pass (Ⓦwww.japanrailpass.net), which must be purchased before arriving in Japan as it's only available to foreign visitors, gives unlimited travel on all except the Nozomi Shinkansen. The 7-day pass costs ¥28,300. The regular second-class fare from Tokyo to Hiroshima is ¥18,550.

14 *SUSHI* AT 300KPH: *RIDING THE* **SHINKANSEN**

Meanwhile, inside the train all is hushed calm. People sleep, punch messages into mobile phones (calls are forbidden), or tuck into *eki-ben*, take-away station meals that are an art form in themselves.

Before you know it, you're pulling in to Kyoto's monumental new station – eyesore or emblem, depending on whom you ask. No time for the city's myriad temples now, though. The doors swoosh shut and you're off again. Osaka brings yet more urban sprawl, but after Kobe the tracks run along the coast, offering tantalizing glimpses of the island-speckled Inland Sea as you near Hiroshima, journey's end.

In a country where cutting-edge design coexists alongside ancient traditions and courtesies, the bullet train is a shining example of the extraordinary attention to detail and awesome teamwork that lies at the heart of Japanese society. Far more than a mere journey, riding the Shinkansen provides a glimpse into what makes Japan tick.

15

ICE COLD
IN AGADEZ:
TRANS-SAHARA
BY MOTORBIKE

Riding across Africa, two stages stand out: the clammy, bug-ridden byways of the Congo Basin – where "infrastructure" is just a good score in Scrabble – and the Sahara. The latter's appeal is uncomplicated: the stark purity of landforms stirred by dawn winds; the simplicity of your daily mission – survival; and the brief serenity of hushed, starlit evenings. It's just you, your bike and the desert.

Disembarking at Algiers it's chaos, but muddle through and by nightfall you'll emerge in the ravines of the Atlas; the desert unrolls before you. By Ghardaia things are warming up and near El Meniaa breathtaking dunes start spilling over the road. Settlements now appear maybe only once a day and so become vital staging posts. Other travellers too acquire a hallowed status: fellow pilgrims on the desert highway.

Some days the road is washed away, submerged in sand or lost in a dust storm, but you soldier on. You pass through the Arak Gorge, a portal to the white sands and granite domes of the haunting Immidir plateau. By now your apprehension has subsided and you dare relax. Within days the volcanic peaks of the Hoggar rise and you roll into Tamanrasset; chugging down the main street you look at the locals and they look back, at a dusty wanderer on a horse with no name.

Like many before you, it's time to focus on the final leg – four days across the long-dreaded *piste* to Agadez. Those first few moments riding the loaded machine on the sands will be a shock but you must be assertive, gunning the throttle across soft patches, resting where you can.

The Niger border is a crossroads: monochrome sobriety meets the colourful exuberance of sub-Saharan Africa. Brightly clothed women mix with mysterious nomads and, for you, an ice-cold beer in the shabby *Hotel Sahara* washes away the desert dust.

need to know

It's best to cross the desert between November and March. You'll find loads of useful information and web links on ⓦwww.adventure-motorcyling.com.

The Karakoram Highway – touted along its length as "The Eighth Wonder of the World" – is the ride of a lifetime for any Himalaya-hungry cyclist. Known to aficionados as the KKH, it was originally a feeder for the fabled Silk Route across Central Asia; today tarmac has replaced goat track, but it still threads its way up from near sea-level in Pakistan to the highest official border crossing in the world – the 4700m Khunjerab Pass into western China.

The highway officially starts in Hassan Abdal, a dusty railroad town west of Pakistan's capital, but if you begin in Islamabad itself, you can finish the first day's ride in Taxila – one of the most significant Buddhist sites in the world. Ahead down the highway lie the plains, where the temperature exceeds a brain-melting 50 °C in summer; in this kind of heat you have to travel when it's coolest, so at the dawn call to prayer, it's time to ride.

The going only gets tougher when you finally reach the hills – these are Himalayan foothills, after all. Now the gauntlet of Indus Kohistan, or 'Valley of the Ungovernables', stands between you and the mountains; here the road teeters hundreds of metres above the raging Indus River and the locals carry guns like handbags. Emerge unscathed and pedal past the roadside Buddha carvings at Chilas as you approach the densest concentration of 8000m mountains in the world: snowy giants such as Nanga Parbat and K2, and picturesque peaks such as Rakaposhi – said to be the most beautiful mountain in the world. The icy breath of glaciers, lying just inches from the road, pushes you up and over Khunjerab Pass, past the Pamirs and down into China's Xinjiang Province for noodles and a dust-down in the desert town of Kashgar.

need to know

The Karakoram Highway runs between Islamabad in Pakistan and Kashgar in China's Xinjiang Province. It takes about a month to cycle the full 1300km; some people start from Gilgit (accessible by air or bus from Islamabad) to avoid the lowland section and knock 500km off the ride. Spring and autumn are the best seasons to ride. Visas are required for both Pakistan and China.

16

1|3|0|0|0

CYCLING THE
KARAKORAM
HIGHWAY

1|2|0|0|0
1|1|0|0|0
1|0|0|0|0
0|9|0|0|0
0|8|0|0|0
0|7|0|0|0
0|6|0|0|0

17 THE PEAK OF PERFECTION

LOUNGING ABOARD THE
GLACIER EXPRESS

The Swiss are often chided for not being much good at, say, football, jokes or wars – but two things they do better than just about anyone are mountains and trains. Combine the two, and you're onto a winner.

We were booked on the Glacier Express; there were pristine blue-skies that morning at St Moritz and our state-of-the-art panoramic carriage awaited. Vast windows extended from knee level right up around the top of the coach; from any seat the views were all-encompassing. As we got going, we didn't feel like passengers, stuck behind glass, but rather travellers, engaged in the scenery.

The journey started under sparkling sunshine beside the River Inn, whose waters tumble east to join the Danube; here, amidst the wild Alpine forests, it's the slenderest of mountain brooks. Every sightline was dominated by sky-blue, snow-white and pine-green. By mid-morning, we were rolling on alongside the young Rhine, crossable here by a single stepping-stone.

As forests, wild gorges, snowy peaks and huddled villages trundled past, the train climbed effortlessly into the bleak high country, above

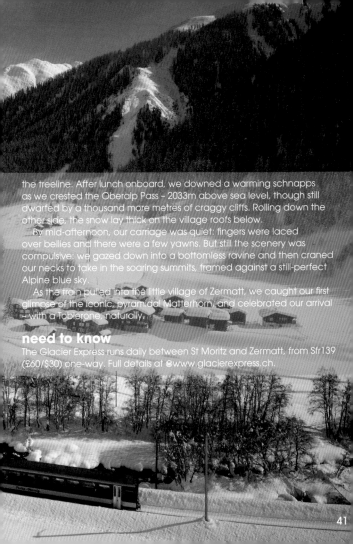

the treeline. After lunch onboard, we downed a warming schnapps as we crested the Oberalp Pass – 2033m above sea level, though still dwarfed by a thousand more metres of craggy cliffs. Rolling down the other side, the snow lay thick on the village roofs below.

By mid-afternoon, our carriage was quiet: fingers were laced over bellies and there were a few yawns. But still the scenery was compulsive: we gazed down into a bottomless ravine and then craned our necks to take in the soaring summits, framed against a still-perfect Alpine blue sky.

As the train pulled into the little village of Zermatt, we caught our first glimpse of the iconic, pyramidal Matterhorn, and celebrated our arrival – with a Toblerone, naturally.

need to know

The Glacier Express runs daily between St Moritz and Zermatt, from Sfr139 (£60/$30) one-way. Full details at @www.glacierexpress.ch.

18

Leaving it All Behind

on the Appalachian Trail

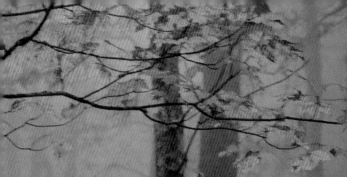

Hiking the Appalachian Trail, the epic trek stretching 2,186 miles from the peak of Springer Mountain in Georgia to the top of Mount Katahdin in Maine, changes your perspective on life, whether you want it to or not. When your house weighs a pound, your job involves walking from sunrise to sunset, and your nights are filled with strangers' stories round roaring campfires, the mundane routines of the modern world are replaced with the realities of survival: water, gear, aching joints, and the insatiable rumbling in your stomach.

A popular saying on the AT is that the only thing that separates a hiker from a hobo is a thin layer of Gore-Tex. So why do so many choose to spend upwards of four months walking a distance that could be covered by a car in two days? Standing on an overlook as you plan your route across the snowcapped peaks of the Smokies at the end of winter, then the indigo waves of the Blue Ridge Mountains in early spring, the grassy green mounds of the Shenandoahs in the heat of mosquito season, and finally the striking profiles of the Presidentials in early fall, you find there's a sublime satisfaction in mapping out your future, one mountain at a time.

But the trail is really about those countless days when you walk twenty-five miles through three thunderstorms and over six mountains, and arrive at your campsite feeling exhausted yet triumphantly alive. That and the sleepy towns to which you hitchhike for supplies, where quirky locals ply you with pitchers of beer at the local bar and blueberry pancakes for breakfast and offer lifts to buy new shoes for the next leg of your trip.

need to know: Every thru-hiker carries two books with them at all times: *The Appalachian Trail Data Book* and *The Appalachian Trail Thru-Hiker's Companion*. Find them both online at @www.appalachiantrail.org.

As the sun slowly dips towards the horizon sometime around 11pm there's nothing better than sitting on deck nursing a warming nightcap as you cruise past mile after gorgeous mile of spruce- and hemlock-choked shoreline. With luck whales will make an appearance; perhaps just a fluke or a tail but maybe a full-body breach. This is Alaska's Inside Passage, flanked by impenetrable snow-capped coastal mountains and incised by hairline fjords that create an interlocking archipelago of over a thousand densely forested islands.

Gliding into port at successive small settlements, you can't help but think these towns insignificant after the large-scale drama of the surrounding landscape. They cling to the few tiny patches of flat land with streets spilling out onto a network of boardwalks over the sea. Shops, streets, and even large salmon canneries are perched picturesquely along the waterside on spruce poles.

Everything is green, courtesy of the low clouds which cloak the surrounding hills and offer frequent rain. But the dripping leaves, sodden mosses, and wispy mist seem to suit ravens and bald eagles. You'll see them everywhere: ravens line up along the railings overlooking the small boat harbours while bald eagles perch, solitary and regal, in the trees above.

The next stop is Glacier Bay National Park, a vast wonderland of ice and barren rock where massive tidewater glaciers push right into the ocean. The ship lingers a few hours here as everyone trains their eyes on the three-mile-wide face where walls of ice periodically crumble away and crash into the iceberg-flecked sea. The schedule is pressing and it is time to move on, but the moment you turn away, the loudest rumble of the day tells you you've just missed the big one.

CRUISING ALASKA'S
INSIDE PASSAGE
19

need to know

Cruise lines such as Celebrity (⊛www.celebritycruises.com) and Holland America (⊛www.hollandamerica.com) run ships carrying up to 2500 passengers. For something more intimate, try CruiseWest (⊛www. cruisewest.com) whose vessels typically carry around 120.

Dunedin's magnificent Victorian railway station is a suitably grand setting for the beginning of our train and cycle journey into the heart of New Zealand's isolated **Maniototo** region. With bikes stashed in the guard's van we board one of the refurbished 1920s wooden carriages of the **Taieri Gorge Railway** and are soon leaving the suburbs behind. The palpable strain on the engine signals the start of the climb into the hinterland, leaving the roads and houses behind. Tunnels burrow though bluffs and steel girder bridges span the gaps, and we hang out on the open footplates between carriages to get a better view.

It's a great trip, but my cycling legs are getting itchy. Two hours later we pull into **Pukerangi**, nothing but a tiny weatherboard stationhouse in the middle of nowhere. Bikes are unloaded and we prepare for the ride ahead: 160km to the town of **Cromwell**. The train has done most of the work for us, and the terrain from here on is fairly flat. This is the **Otago Central Rail Trail**, which loops through the Maniototo region, an open expanse of three shallow valleys separated by the Lammerlaw and the **Rock** and **Pillar** ranges.

When the trains stopped coming to these parts the region entered terminal decline, but the popularity of the rail trail has changed all that. Wanting to show our appreciation we're tempted to stop at one of the revitalized country pubs, but instead follow a sign off the trail to a little shop selling homemade

PUKERANGI

need to know

The Taieri Gorge Railway (services daily; ☎03/477 4449, ⊛www.taieri.co.nz; NZ$42/£15 one way) runs from from Dunedin to Pukerangi, where you start on the Otago Central Rail Trail (⊛www.centralotagorailtrail. co.nz). You can rent bikes for NZ$35/£12 a day from Cycle Surgery (☎07/477-7473) either in Dunedin or in Middlemarch and drop them at Cromwell.

cakes and great espresso. Life is good.

For our second night on the trail we'll
stay in a comfortable B&B, but tonight
we've opted for some rustic,
converted shearers' quarters.
They're still 30km ahead,
so we get back on our
bikes and start
the pedals
spinning.

20 Riding into the heart of the Maniototo

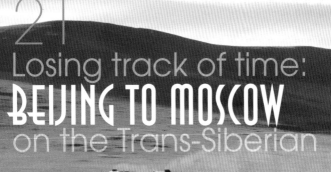

21
Losing track of time:
BEIJING TO MOSCOW
on the Trans-Siberian

need to know
A ticket from Beijing to Moscow costs around US$400 (£200) through a travel agency; you can buy the ticket yourself for around US$200 (£100) at the CITS office in the Beijing International Hotel, but you'll have to get a transit visa for Russia as well, which can be a hassle.

On the fourth day I stopped caring about time. I thought it was the fourth day, in fact it was the third. Beijing was a receding memory, Moscow impossibly distant. I had slipped into the habit of sleeping for four hours and then getting up for four hours, it didn't matter whether it was light or dark. Life inside the train bore no relation to the outside world – Siberia – which barreled past, cold, unwelcoming and as predictable as wallpaper: birch trees, hills, birch trees, plains, birch trees.

'I hate those trees', said the elderly German in my compartment, 'I want to cut them all down.'

Occasionally we passed an untidy village of wooden cabins but mostly the only human touch to the epic landscape was the telegraph poles at the side of the track.

My first Russian was a young guy in a shell suit with a moustache and an anarchy tattoo. 'The 'Beatles', he said, on hearing I was British.

'The Rolling Stones', I countered.

He nodded 'The Doors.'

'Pearl Jam?' I inquired.

'Nirvana,' he asserted. 'Napalm Death.'

Once or twice a day the train stopped and I'd emerge for fresh air, dizzy and blinking, onto a platform swarming with frenzied shoppers. Traders stood in the carriage door and the townsfolk, who had waited all week for two minutes of consumerism, rioted to get to them. To save time the traders threw money over their shoulders into the corridor to be collected by colleagues. They sold world cup t-shirts, plastic jewellery and Mickey Mouse umbrellas. Even the man from the dining car had a cupboard of trainers, which was perhaps why he could only offer gherkins and soup in his official capacity.

I played cards then slept, battleships, slept, charades, slept. It was an invalid's life – a long slow delirium in comfortable confinement. But on the seventh day, or perhaps the sixth, when grey housing blocks started appearing and Moscow was imminent, I suddenly felt nostalgic for that easy sloth. When I finally got off, something felt terribly wrong; it took me a while to figure it out – oh yes, the ground wasn't moving.

22 Biking

With its record breaking heat, long stretches of barren desert, crazed feral dogs and frantic Mexican truck drivers, the pothole-riddled Transpeninsular Highway that runs a thousand miles through Mexico's Baja California is one of the greatest pedal-powered road trips in the world.

Turning your back on the skyscrapers of San Diego and cycling across the heavily guarded no-man's-land into the dusty, litter strewn streets of Tijuana, you may as well be entering a new world. New smells, new language, new rules – your Mexican cycling adventure is underway.

Leaving Tijuana, the highway begins along the Pacific coast with its crashing waves and perfect sunsets, but it soon leads inland to the dry heat of the unforgiving Desierto de Vizcaíno. Here, days of gruelling climbs in sun-baked surrounds and nights camped amongst the cactus and coyotes are eventually rewarded with the mirage-like vision of San Ignacio. This sixteenth-

the **Baja**

need to know
A leisurely ride from Tijuana to La Paz with plenty of rest days will take around a month; it's best done between October and March as summer temperatures in the desert are often above 100˚F/38˚C.

century Jesuit Mission, built around the cool, palm-lined waters of a natural oasis, is a perfect rest stop for lounging in the shade of the bougainvillea and refuelling on sticky, energy-packed local dates. Back in the saddle, you re-enter the desert, riding through the forests of giant Cardon cacti and Boojum trees that stretch endlessly towards the distant blue mountains beyond.

Limping into La Paz, after the best part of a month on the road, your journey through the Baja is almost complete. All that remains is to grab a couple of fish tacos and a cold bottle of Pacifico and head to the waterfront *malecón* to watch your last spectacular Baja sunset.

CRUISING THE
COOLEST COAST
IN EUROPE

For over one hundred years, the Hurtigrute boat service has made the dramatic voyage from Bergen in the western fjords of Norway to Kirkenes, deep within the Arctic Circle and hard up against the Russian border. It's a beautiful trawl up the Norwegian coast, past towering peaks and deep-blue fjords, the views growing more spectacular with every passing knot.

This is far from your average cruise. Quoits are distinctly absent from the upper deck and there are no afternoon salsa classes with the crew; entertainment comes, instead, in the form of the pounding ocean and some truly staggering scenery. The Hurtigrute calls in at thirty-five ports on the way – some are thriving cities steeped in maritime history, others little more than a jetty and a cluster of uniform wooden houses painted in the ubiquitous red. Joining the boat at Bodø in the far north of Norway you're ensured a spectacular start.

Easing gently out of Bodø and into the Norwegian Sea, the boat turns starboard for the Lofoten Islands, the soaring crags of the Lofotenveggen – a jagged wall of mountains that stretches 160km along its shore – looming ever closer. Hopping in and out of a couple of rustic fishing villages along the coast, it then squeezes through the Vesterålen Islands, almost rubbing its bows along the sheer cliff faces that line the Trollfjord, before pushing on to Tromsø, a teeming metropolis compared to the sparse settlements left behind.

From here, the Hurtigrute sets off on its final leg, stopping for a couple of hours at Nordkaap, a desolate spot that marks the northernmost point in mainland Europe, before traversing the Barents Sea. Finally, six days after leaving Bergen and 67 hours from Bodø, it triumphantly chugs into Kirkenes, concrete proof – after such a journey – that it is often better to travel than to arrive.

need to know

Fares for the journey from Bergen to Kirkenes start at around £450/$845 (including meals); shorter hops between ports – such as the trip from Bodø to Kirkenes – are significantly cheaper. See ⓦwww.hurtigruten.com for sailing schedules and to book online.

Brazil's Royal Road

To travel along the Estrada Real feels like taking a step back in time. This "Royal Road", commissioned by the Portuguese Crown in 1697 to provide access to the gold- and gem-rich mountains, stretches 1000km through Brazil's interior. Wending its way from the small colonial-era port of Paraty in the south through former mining outposts all the way to Diamantina, a town deep in the Brazilian highlands, the road fell into disuse after the end of the Gold Rush a century or so later; in recent years, however, the route has experienced something of a renaissance, with visitors drawn by the fine colonial architecture and old-world feel of its communities as well as the unspoiled, bucolic scenery it takes in.

With time and determination, you can walk the length of the Estrada Real, but most just choose a small section for leisurely exploration. Hiking up the steep and often slippery 12km stretch of the original cobblestone surface from Paraty you'll enter the Serra do Mar, the rainforest-covered mountain range separating the coast from the interior. Here hummingbirds hover at brightly coloured flowers and monkeys swing from branches overhead. As you trudge deeper into the forest, sharing the road with pack mules headed for isolated farmsteads, you can stop for a refreshing dip in a series of cascading waterfalls. Further on, you'll be rewarded by a sign pointing towards a simple pousada – a country inn – with spectacular views of Paraty and the ocean beyond.

The further north one travels along the Estrada Real, the more parched the landscape becomes. The 60km stretch linking Diamantina and Serro, for example, appears positively lunar; yet even in its most abandoned sections the road shelters oasis-like hamlets whose enterprising locals have caught on to the benefits of tourism. Stop off at a roadside stall for a bottle of home-produced cachaça (a sugar-based fire-water) or to sample fresh Minas cheese. If you're not in a hurry, stay over in a pousada and feast on the local cuisine: rich, greasy and incredibly tasty pork, jerked-beef, beans and rice, all cooked in traditional fashion, on wood-burning stoves.

need to know: Dozens of local agencies have sprung up to help visitors experience the Estrada Real. Although only in Portuguese, @www.estradareal.org.br offers local information and contacts. On the stretch of Estrada Real outside of Paraty, see @www.caminhodoouro.com.br. For accommodation between Diamantina and Serro, see @www.pousadarecantodovale.com.br and @www.pousadarefugio5amigos.com.br.

There's something deeply alluring about travelling somewhere you can't reach by car – a truly remote place, far from anywhere. The tiny settlement of Churchill, shivering by the shores of the great Hudson Bay in Canada's far north, is just such a place; its only connection to the rest of the world is a thousand-mile-long railway that begins in the prairie town of Winnipeg. You start your journey in the agricultural heartland of Canada and end it in a frozen wasteland where only arctic mosses and lichen can grow. It's a startling transformation – a real journey to the edge of the world.

The train itself – the Hudson Bay – oozes character with its 1950s stainless steel carriages, polished chrome fixtures and old-fashioned dining car. This is the place to get chatting to your fellow travellers, among them gnarled fishermen and trappers, Cree and Chipewyan natives and even a few Inuit. Most of them know this land like the back of their hands, and will readily tell you the names of the flora and fauna passing by. They'll also fill you in on the minor scandals attached to the various communities along the line: the embezzling mayor who ended his days trapping furs to earn his crusts; the village where a Mountie was shot dead by a Cree outlaw a hundred years ago.

The journey includes two nights on the train; waking up from your second night, pull open the blind and you'll feel like you're on another planet: gone are the verdant forests of yesterday, replaced by stunted, shrivelled stumps which peter out altogether as you enter the Barren Lands – a region of fierce winds, bitter cold and permanently frozen soil. And then you pull in to Churchill and the phrase: "end of the line" takes on a whole new meaning. Way up here, in Canada's subarctic, you'll feel farther from civilization than you ever thought possible.

need to know

Operated by VIA Rail (@www.viarail.ca), the Hudson Bay train runs from Winnipeg to Churchill three days a week. One-way economy class tickets cost from CDN$141 (£63), with private bedrooms from CDN$327 (£145).

25

Redefining Remote on the *Hudson Bay* *Train*

25

Ultimate
experiences
Journeys
miscellany

1 The first intercontinental journey

Humans migrated from Asia to the Americas twelve thousand years ago across the 1600-kilometre-long Bering Land Bridge, which connected Siberia to Alaska during the Pleistocene Ice Ages.

 # 2 Derivations

English has a number of words to do with journeys, many of which have undertaken a journey of their own, into the language from foreign tongues. "Journey" itself derives from the Old French journée, meaning "a day's travel". Other journey-related words include "trip", from the Low German trippen ("to stamp"); "voyage", from the Latin viaticum ("provision for travel") via the Old French veiage; and "trek", from the Afrikaans/Middle Dutch trekken ("to travel").

 # 3 Five space journeys

1957: The dog Laika becomes the first living creature to be sent into space.

1961: First man in space: Yuri Gagarin.

1963: First woman in space: Valentina Tereshkova.

1969: First moon landing.

2001: First space tourist: Dennis Tito spends seven days on the International Space Station.

"The gladdest moment in human life is the departure upon a distant journey into unknown lands."

Sir Richard F. Burton

4 The journey to the roof of the world

Attaining the summit of Mount Everest, the world's highest peak at 8848m, is the **ultimate mountaineering challenge**. In 1953, Sir Edmund Hillary and Tenzing Norgay were the first people to complete the ascent. Other Everest records include the first ascent by a woman (in 1975), the first ascent without oxygen supplies (1978), the first descent on skis (2000), and the first ascent by a blind person (2001). Climbing Everest has now become something of an aspiration for wealthy professionals – the current going rate for the venture is just under $55,000/£30,000.

However scaling Everest is a dangerous endeavor and at the close of 2004, 179 people had lost their lives in the attempt, a fatality rate of nine percent. About one-third of the total deaths is comprised of the local Sherpa population, many of whom serve as guides. For them, Everest has spiritual significance and there are many taboos relating to it, one of which is a ban on sex for anyone attempting the summit – it is thought to bring bad luck.

 # 5 A journeys playlist

Route 66 **Chuck Berry**

Highway Star **Deep Purple**

Come Fly With Me **Frank Sinatra**

Last Train to Clarksville **The Monkees**

Do You Know The Way to San José **Dionne Warwick**

Leaving On A Jet Plane **Peter, Paul and Mary**

Highway 61 Revisited **Bob Dylan**

Trans Europe Express **Kraftwerk**

On The Road Again **Willie Nelson**

I Still Haven't Found What I'm Looking For **U2**

6 Five literary journeys

The Canterbury Tales by Geoffrey Chaucer. The story of a group of pilgrims who regale each other with interesting tales as they travel.

The Lord of the Rings by J.R.R. Tolkien. Tolkien's landmark trilogy, part war novel, part quasi-historical saga, focuses on Frodo's arduous quest to destroy the One Ring in Mount Doom.

The Adventure's of Huckleberry Finn by Mark Twain. Raft down the river with Huck and Tom as they grapple with slavery and discover friendship in the deep south.

Dante's **Inferno**. Dante's allegorical journey through the nine circles of hell.

On the Road by Jack Kerouac. Beat Generation travels across America that make you want to get out there and hit the road yourself.

"One of the pleasantest things in the world is going on a journey; but I like to go by myself."

William Hazlitt

7 Up, up and away

Orville and Wilbur Wright are generally credited with building the world's first heavier-than-air aircraft, in 1903; their first flight covered all of **37 metres**. Aeronautical technology took off amazingly quickly, so much so that six years later, Louis Blériot managed the first crossing of the English Channel by plane. The first commercial jet aircraft, the De Havilland Comet, went into service in the 1950s, and commercial supersonic flights arrived in the mid-1970s, thanks to Concorde. The new frontier for airborne travel today is to reach for the stars: Richard Branson's Virgin Galactic venture plans to offer spaceflights to the paying public.

8 Railways

The first **trains** were pulled by horses; steam-powered trains didn't come along until the early nineteenth century. The first public passenger service opened in 1825, connecting Stockton and Darlington in northeast England. By the end of the nineteenth century, rail travel was widespread. Today, the USA has the world's most extensive rail network, with 233,800km of track – ironic considering it has so few long-distance passenger trains – while the Japanese travel further by train than any other nationality: 1891km per person per year.

9 Five historical routes

Appian Way This most famous of all Roman roads ran from Rome to Brindisi and was the principal route for the Roman army through the Republic; military bases were stationed along its length.

The Oregon Trail From the 1830s until the 1860s, thousands of American migrants travelled west in covered wagon trains to the wilds of Oregon and California, lured by offers of free land and the promise of a better life.

The Silk Road A celebrated caravan route between China and the ports of the Black and Mediterranean seas, the Silk Road flourished as a corridor for trade from 150 BC to the mid-seventeenth century.

The Clipper Route The fastest round-the-world sailing route, named for its use by clipper ships sailing between Europe and the Far East, Australia and New Zealand.

The Grand Trunk Road One of South Asia's oldest major roads, for centuries serving as the main artery across northern India. As with many key roads, it had a strategic significance, facilitating not only trade but also incursions by the Afghans and Persians, and the British colonization of India.

"For my part, I travel not to go anywhere, but to go. I travel for travel's sake. The great affair is to move."

Robert Louis Stevenson

10 Car crazy

When the first **automobiles** appeared, they were so terrifying to the general public that a flag-waving youth was required to run ahead of each car and warn of its approach. But soon, with Oldsmobile pioneering the mass-produced and affordably-priced automobile, cars became commonplace and in 2002 there were nearly 600 million passenger cars in the world. Perhaps surprisingly, Lebanon is the country with the highest number of cars relative to its population – 732 vehicles for every 1,000 inhabitants.

11 A trial of Endurance

Sir Ernest Henry Shackleton embarked on a daring expedition in 1914 when, on his ship the **Endurance**, he attempted to sail around the coast of Antartica, between the Weddell and Ross seas. This goal had to be abandoned when the ship was crushed by sea ice short of the continent. Shackleton then led his crew on an epic 639-day journey by sledge and boat to Elephant Island, just off the Antarctic Peninsula. From here he sailed with some of the men to South Georgia Island in the Falklands, where help was sought. Miraculously, everyone was rescued.

12 The New World

Though Christopher Columbus is generally credited with being the first European explorer to set foot in the **New World**, it was in fact the Vikings who first "discovered" the North American coast, around 1000 AD. However, their exploration had little effect as they didn't settle there; it wasn't until Columbus made landfall in the Bahamas in 1492 that European involvement in the Americas began. Full-fledged colonization followed, resulting in the deracination of many native American populations and their decimation from diseases introduced by the Europeans.

Inventing the wheel

No invention has had a greater impact on man's ability to conquer distance than the **wheel**, which came into use in Mesopotamia during the Neolithic Age. The earliest vehicles had one axle and were used like a wheelbarrow. Around 2000 BC the Egyptians discovered that using spoked wheels allowed the construction of lighter, swifter vehicles, such as the chariot. The wheel evolved little in subsequent millennia; it wasn't until 1888 that John Dunlop, a British vet, invented the tyre, which made travel much more comfortable by cushioning bumps in the road.

 # Five trailblazers

Marco Polo (1254–1324) Venetian merchant who explored China at the end of the thirteenth century. His book about his travels made him the most famous explorer of his time.

Ibn Battuta (1304–69) The greatest traveller of the ancient and medieval worlds, this Moroccan legal scholar spent 24 years meandering through the Middle and Far East.

Vasco da Gama (c. 1469–1525) The first person to sail directly from Europe to India, around the Cape of Good Hope. His voyage was the harbinger of Portugese colonial rule in Goa.

James Cook (1728–79) An English explorer and cartographer, Cook "discovered" and claimed Australia for the British, and was also the first European to set foot in the Hawaiian Islands.

David Livingstone (1813–73) A Scottish missionary, Livingstone was one of the first Westerners to cross the African continent and searched, unsuccessfully, for the source of the Nile.

The Grand Tour

In the eighteenth century it was common for **young British aristocrats** to take an extended educational tour through Europe, intended to broaden their horizons, hone their language skills and cultivate "taste". Participants were mostly aged between 18 and 20, and were accompanied by a tutor or companion who was meant to guide their studies and protect them from base temptations; most tutors failed miserably at both.

 # Five journeys on the big screen

Lawrence of Arabia (1962). The plot of this Oscar-winning film, based on the life of T.E. Lawrence and starring Peter O'Toole, follows Lawrence's experiences and adventures in the Arabian desert during World War I.

Monty Python and the Holy Grail (1975). King Arthur and his knights search for the Holy Grail, fending off improbable foes such as a three-headed giant and a murderous rabbit.

Star Wars (1977). Luke Skywalker's epic journey from his home planet to save Princess Leia and the world from the grips of Darth Vader.

The Motorcycle Diaries (2004). Based on his journals, this is the tale of young Che Guevara's motorcycle journey through South America in the 1950s.

Thelma and Louise (1991). The ultimate chick flick: two housewives escape their dull suburban lives to go on a rebellious road trip that takes a turn for the worse.

"Journeys end in lovers meeting
Every wise man's son doth know."

Shakespeare's *Twelfth Night*

 # Five mythical destinations

Atlantis This legendary lost continent, believed to have sunk in an apocalyptic disaster thousands of years ago, has had dozens of reputed locations.

The Isles of the Blessed According to early medieval Irish Christians, these islands were an earthly paradise, supposedly discovered by St Brendan the Navigator and located in the western Atlantic.

El Dorado A legendary city of gold, El Dorado was thought to be located in various mountainous, jungled areas of South America. Its myth lured countless European explorers to the continent in the sixteenth and early seventeenth centuries.

The Fountain of Youth The Spaniard Juan Ponce de Léon invested many years in a futile search for a spring whose waters brought eternal youth, word of which was picked up from natives of Cuba and Puerto Rico by the earliest Spanish explorers.

Shambala According to Tibetan Buddhist tradition, a mystical kingdom called Shambala ("Place of Peace") lies hidden somewhere beyond the Himalayas, and can be reached only by those with the appropriate karma.

 # Four legs good

Throughout history the **horse** has been the animal most widely used for getting around, but many other four-legged forms of transport have been deployed from time to time – with varying degrees of success. In frozen climes, **huskies** or sled dogs provide an invaluable mode of transport, while **camels**, since their domestication around 2500 BC, have made it possible for humans undertake long journeys through arid areas. **Elephants**, however, need too much food and tire far too easily to be practical as people-carriers. This didn't stop Hannibal from invading Italy in 218 BC by crossing the Pyrenees and the Alps with elephants; only one of his 37 pachyderms survived the trek.

The hippie trail

The Sixties and Seventies saw travellers follow the so-called **hippie trail** overland from Europe to East Asia, with Turkey, Iran, Afghanistan, Pakistan, India and Nepal as the way stations. Seeking a more authentic experience than the package tours their parents took, most of these travellers sought to connect with local culture, including indigenous dress. This had a major impact on European fashion houses: colourful, flowing garments and ethnic jewellery were soon seen on the catwalks of Milan and Paris.

"Never go on trips with anyone you do not love."

Ernest Hemingway

 # Five holy journeys

The Stations of the Cross Christian pilgrims in Jerusalem visit each of the fourteen Stations of the Cross – locations where key events leading up to Jesus's crucifixion took place. Many people even drag a wooden cross on their back, as Jesus did.

The Hajj The pilgrimage to Mecca that takes place in the last month of the Muslim calendar. Pilgrims are required to wear special white robes and refrain from acts such as the cutting of their fingernails and sexual intercourse for the duration.

Circling Mount Kailash Located in the Trans-Himalayas in Tibet, this mountain is the sacred site to four religions: Hinduism, Buddhism, Jainism and the Bon faith. Pilgrims believe that a ritual walk around Kailash brings good fortune; the most devout attempt the 50km in a single day.

A pilgrimage to Lourdes In the southwest of France, Lourdes is home to one of the world's most famous Marian shrines, and to a spring whose waters are thought to have great healing properties; the Catholic Church has recognized dozens of miracle healings at the site.

Nhlangakazi Each January this mountain, in South Africa's KwaZulu-Natal province, is the scene for ritual dances by thousands of members of the Shembe church, which preaches a hybrid of Christian and Zulu beliefs.

21 Les Voyages Extraordinaires

The French author Jules Verne (1828–1905) brought futuristic modes of travel into literature and so became a pioneer of science fiction genre. In his *A Journey to the Centre of the Earth*, a professor and his nephew travel down through an Icelandic volcano to the earth's core, while in *From the Earth to the Moon*, members of an American gun club build a craft, propelled by explosives, which they board and then fire at the moon – only to end up trapped in lunar orbit.

 # 22 Wayfaring conquerors

Some of history's greatest **conquerors** ranged far and wide in pursuit of their aims. Alexander the Great (356–323BC), from the Greek province of Macedonia, spread Hellenic culture throughout the Middle East. In his lifetime he conquered the entire Persian Empire, extending his own empire as far as the Punjab before turning west where he had planned, before his death, to conquer Europe. Under Trajan (53–117), one of Rome's foremost military commanders and conquerors, the Roman empire attained its greatest extent, including Mesopotamia and Arabia and even reaching into Persia. One of the most successful and ruthless military leaders of all time was, of course, Genghis Khan (1162–1227), who invaded and conquered territory from Turkey through Russia to China; in so doing, he founded the Mongol empire, the largest contiguous empire in world history.

"How does it feel
To be without a home
Like a complete unknown
Like a rolling stone?"

Bob Dylan

23 Out of body, out of mind

Meditation is practised in most Eastern belief systems, often as a way of disconnecting from the outside world and undertaking metaphysical journeys of the soul. Through Transcendental Meditation, a state of pure consciousness is supposed to be achieved, in which the mind is not connected to terrestrial reality. Astral Travel, sometimes attained via lucid dreaming, meditation or the use of psychotropic drugs, is regarded as involving an astral body which moves along with the physical body but exists in a parallel world called the astral plane.

> *"I always love to begin a journey on Sundays, because I shall have the prayers of the church, to preserve all that travel by land, or by water."*
>
> **Jonathan Swift**

 # 24 Protectors

Many cultures and faiths invoke the **protection** of a particular deity or saint at the beginning of a journey. The ancient Greeks looked to Hermes, the son of Zeus, for aid; attired in winged sandals and a winged hat, he was not only their messenger of the Gods but also the god of travel. In Aztec mythology there is a god of travellers, Yacatecuhtli, whose name means "he who goes before". Hindus generally begin any enterprise, particularly travel, by invoking the mischievous but shrewd god of wisdom and good fortune, Ganesha. For Catholics, St Christopher is the patron saint of travellers and also the protector of the dying, linking journeys in life to those after death.

25 Classical journeys

The two most famous **epic poems** of antiquity are Homer's *Odyssey*, relating the ten-year journey of Odysseus back to his native Ithaca and his wife Penelope after the fall of Troy, and Virgil's *Aeneid*, following Aeneas in his wanderings from Troy to the shores of Italy. A hallmark of both works is the tenaciousness of their main protagonists, who overcome all obstacles – from the wrath of the gods to attacks by terrifying beasts such as the Cyclops – to achieve their goals.

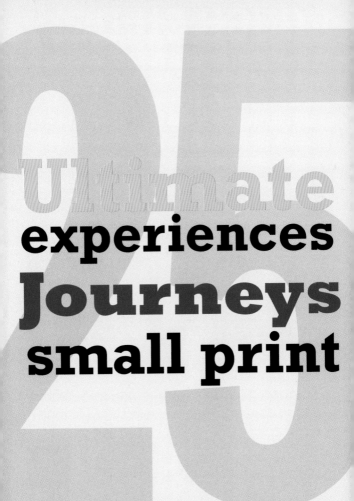

25 Ultimate experiences

Journeys

small print

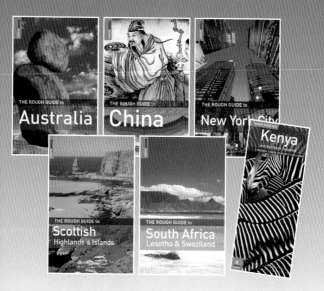

ROUGH GUIDES – don't just travel

We hope you've been inspired by the experiences in this book. To us, they sum up what makes travelling such an extraordinary and stimulating experience. There are 24 other books in the 25 Ultimate Experiences series, each conceived to whet your appetite for travel and for everything the world has to offer. As well as covering the globe, the 25s series also includes books on **World Food, Adventure Travel, Places to Stay, Ethical Travel, Wildlife Adventures** and **Wonders of the World**.

When you start planning your trip, Rough Guides' new-look guides, maps and phrasebooks are the ultimate companions. For 25 years we've been refining what makes a good guidebook and we now include more colour photos and more information – on average 50% more pages – than any of our competitors. Just look for the sky-blue spines.

Rough Guides don't just travel – we also believe in getting the most out of life without a passport. Since the publication of the bestselling Rough Guides to **The Internet** and **World Music**, we've brought out a wide range of lively and authoritative guides on everything from **Climate Change** to **Hip-Hop**, from **MySpace** to **Film Noir** and from **The Brain** to **The Rolling Stones**.

Publishing information

Rough Guide 25 Ultimate experiences Journeys Published May 2007 by Rough Guides Ltd, 80 Strand, London WC2R 0RL
345 Hudson St, 4th Floor, New York, NY 10014, USA
14 Local Shopping Centre, Panchsheel Park, New Delhi 110017, India
Distributed by the Penguin Group
Penguin Books Ltd,
80 Strand, London WC2R 0RL
Penguin Group (USA)
375 Hudson Street, NY 10014, USA
Penguin Group (Australia)
250 Camberwell Road, Camberwell, Victoria 3124, Australia
Penguin Books Canada Ltd,
10 Alcorn Avenue, Toronto, Ontario, Canada M4V 1E4
Penguin Group (NZ)
67 Apollo Drive, Mairangi Bay, Auckland 1310, New Zealand
Printed in China
© Rough Guides 2007

80pp
A catalogue record for this book is available from the British Library
ISBN: 978-1-8435-3831-8

The publishers and authors have done their best to ensure the accuracy and currency of all the information in Rough Guide 25 Ultimate experiences Journeys, however, they can accept no responsibility for any loss, injury, or inconvenience sustained by any traveller as a result of information or advice contained in the guide.

1   3   5   7   9   8   6   4   2

Rough Guide credits

Editor: Sarah Eno
Design & picture research: Link Hall, Jj Luck
Cartography: Maxine Repath, Katie Lloyd-Jones
Cover design: Diana Jarvis, Chloë Roberts
Production: Aimee Hampson, Katherine Owers
Proofreader: Lucy White

The authors

Keith Drew (Experiences 1, 23) is a senior editor for Rough Guides.

Richard Trillo (Experiences 2, 10) is the author of the *Rough Guide to Kenya* and the co-author of Rough Guides to West Africa and the Gambia.

Chris Scott (Experiences 3, 15) is a contributor to the *Rough Guide to Australia* and writes books on adventure motorcycling.

Brendon Griffin (Experience 4) has contributed to Rough Guides on Spain, Portugal, West Africa and Central America.

Alice Park (Experience 5) is a travel editor for Rough Guides.

Jeff Cranmer (Experience 6) is the co-author of the *Rough Guide to Laos*.

Melissa Graham (Experience 7, 25) is the co-author of Rough Guides to Ecuador and Chile.

Lily Hyde (Experience 8) has travelled extensively as a journalist in Eastern Europe.

Donald Reid (Experience 9) is the co-author of the *Rough Guide to Scotland*.

Helena Smith (Experience 11) is an editor, author and photographer who has contributed to many Rough Guides including those on her native Scotland.

Jean McNeill (Experience 12) is the author of the *Rough Guide to Costa Rica*.

Lily Fink (Experience 13) cruised the Panama canal in 1999. She lives in New York.

Jan Dodd (Experience 14) is the co-author of Rough Guides to Japan and Vietnam.

Laura Stone (Experience 16) has crossed and re-crossed the Himalaya by bicycle.

Matthew Teller (Experience 17) is the author of the *Rough Guide to Switzerland*.

Sara Lieber (Experience 18) hiked the 2000-mile-plus length of the Appalachian trail in 2002.

Paul Whitfield (Experiences 19, 20) is the author of the *Rough Guide to Alaska* and contributes to the *Rough Guide to New Zealand*.

Simon Lewis (Experience 21) is the author of the *Rough Guide to Beijing* and is co-author of the *Rough Guide to China*.

Tom Kevill-Davies (Experience 22), also known as "the hungry cyclist", set off to pedal the world in search of the perfect meal in May 2005.

Oliver Marshall (Experience 24) is a co-author of the *Rough Guide to Brazil*.

Sarah Eno (Miscellany) is a travel editor for Rough Guides.

Picture credits

Over 70 reference books and hundreds of travel
guides, maps & phrasebooks that cover the world

Australia

Cuba

Britain

Singapore

Vietnam

New York City

Morocco

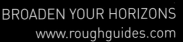

Index